A POETRY COLLECTION

BROKEN TRUST BURNING WORLD

A bold and unapologetic collection of poems
that critically examine societal norms,
challenge popular ideologies, and question
the narratives shaping today's world

DREW MACKBY SAND

Broken Trust, Burning World © by Drew Mackby Sand 2024.

All rights reserved. No portion of this book may be reproduced, distributed, stored in a retrieval system, or transmitted in any form or by any means—electronic, mechanical, photocopying, recording, or otherwise—without prior written permission from the publisher, except for brief quotations used in reviews, articles, or scholarly works.

This book is intended for artistic and expressive purposes only. It is not a source of professional advice or guidance and should not be relied upon as such.

First Edition 2024
A catalogue record of this book is with the Library & Archives Canada.

Independently Published
Names: Drew Mackby Sand
Title: Broken Trust, Burning World
Identifiers: ISBN 978-1-0690582-1-8

CONTENTS

INTRODUCTION 7

THE AWAKENING 9

- Realization and betrayal—poems uncovering truth amid the world's lies and manipulation.

MACHINES OF GREED 37

- Corporations, billionaires, and the exploitation machine.

CORRUPT THRONES 61

- Betrayal and corruption by officials, policymakers, unelected authorities, and their collaborators.

FALSE PROPHETS 83

- Disdain for ideologues, fearmongers, and mindless conformity.

SILENT REVOLT 105

- Personal grief, inner rebellion, and a burning desire for change.

I just wanted to express myself

INTRODUCTION

Welcome to *Broken Trust, Burning World*—a collection born from the fire of disillusionment and the relentless search for truth. These poems are raw, unapologetic reflections of a world unraveling, offering both critique and defiance in the face of conformity. They explore societal collapse, individual resistance, and the human spirit's enduring will to rise above manipulation and decay.

Broken Trust, Burning World is a powerful and unapologetic collection of poems that confronts the complexities of modern society. In these raw and stirring verses, the author delves into the tension between prevailing ideologies and the individual's quest for truth, freedom, and authenticity. With a critical eye, the poems challenge mainstream narratives, question political and social structures, and examine the impact of groupthink, media manipulation, and cultural division.

This collection is not for those seeking comfort in popular views. It speaks directly to those willing to question the status quo, challenge conventional wisdom, and explore controversial perspectives. From the broken promises of a rapidly changing world to the disillusionment with societal systems, *Broken Trust, Burning World* is a journey through the frustrations and revelations of those who refuse to simply accept what they are told.

If you are open to provocative, uncomfortable truths and are ready to confront the deeper layers of today's social, political, and cultural landscape, this book is for you. But be warned—these poems are designed to provoke, stir, and challenge. *Broken Trust, Burning World* is a work that will leave you questioning, reflecting, and perhaps even redefining what you thought you knew.

DISCLAIMER FOR THE "BROKEN TRUST, BURNING WORLD" POETRY COLLECTION

The contents of this poetry collection, including all written works, reflect the personal opinions, thoughts, and artistic expressions of the author. The views and beliefs expressed are those of the author alone and are intended for creative, intellectual, and expressive purposes. This work does not aim to defame, harm, or discriminate against any individual, group, or entity. Any similarities between the poems and real persons, living or dead, are purely coincidental.

The poems are intended as artistic and literary works, and as such, they represent a form of protected speech under the constitutional right to free expression. The inclusion of controversial topics, societal criticisms, and political commentary is not intended to incite hate, violence, or illegal activities, but rather to provoke thought, challenge prevailing narratives, and promote individual reflection.

The author reserves the right to express opinions and engage in societal commentary through the medium of poetry. These opinions are not intended as factual statements or declarations, but are artistic devices aimed at exploring various perspectives, ideologies, and emotional responses to contemporary issues. The works are not intended to incite any form of unlawful activity or encourage any harmful behavior. Readers are reminded that these poems should not be taken literally but should be understood as creative expressions of personal perspective, metaphor, and artistic reflection.

By publishing this collection, the author acknowledges the complex and sensitive nature of some of the topics discussed, and any misunderstanding of the work's intent should be viewed within the context of artistic freedom and the right to engage in cultural dialogue.

To the fullest extent permitted by law, the author asserts that the publication of this collection is a protected act of free speech and expression. The author cannot be held liable for the opinions expressed in this work, nor will liability be assumed for any potential misinterpretation, misrepresentation, or wrongful accusation resulting from the contents herein.

THE AWAKENING

Realization and betrayal—poems uncovering truth amid the world's lies and manipulation.

THE AWAKENING

Red Flags in a World of Masks

Once you see the truth,
The masks fall—
What was hidden, distorted,
Becomes plain.

Facts should be known,
Common—
But instead, they've been bent, twisted,
Fed to us as lies.

Suddenly, you see
How deep the damage runs—
How narcissism breathes
In every corner of this world.

You see the manipulation,
Fragile egos clothed in false virtue.
People wearing identities like armor,
Weapons forged in division—
Splitting communities
With promises of safety,
Of righteousness.

They stand on pedestals,
Patting themselves on the back,
Blind to the chaos
Beneath their feet.

These are not the spiritual—
They are far from it.
Their moral authority is hollow,

THE AWAKENING

An illusion built on lies.

They preach,
They manipulate,
As predators do,
Posing as saints.

They spread seeds of division
While claiming unity,
Sowing hate in the name of good.

And once you see it,
You cannot unsee it.
It's everywhere—
So blatant,
So unbearable—

And you wonder
How others cannot see.
They cling to falsehoods,
Built on ego—
And the gap between you and them
Widens.

It's hard to exist in this world now,
Hard to connect
When all around you are red flags—
Waving bright and violent—
When all you want
Is to stay far away
From the epidemic of lies
That has swallowed so many whole.

THE AWAKENING

Lessons in Chains

They said: Learn what we preach, not to think for yourself—
And chained our minds to hollow creeds.
History became a courtroom,
Where the living stand trial for the dead.

Faces inked in textbooks—
Saints and sinners pre-assigned.
"Truth" no longer questioned,
Only recited in trembling tones.

We inherit crimes we never committed,
Wear guilt like a branded skin.
This is not learning—
It's indoctrination masked as justice.

THE AWAKENING

The Narcissist's Playbook

Be seen. Be praised. Be envied.
Be anything but real.

Apologize if it gains you favor—
Strike if it brings you power.
Wear virtue like a mask—
Discard when no one's watching.

THE AWAKENING

Convenience Kills

They made it easy—
Grab, pay, swallow, forget.
But convenience comes coated
In cancer and lies.

Fast fixes, slow deaths—
We chose ease over effort.
But now I see:
Effort is survival.

THE AWAKENING

Inherited Fires

Born into a world already burning,
They hand us ashes and call them history.
"Hold this," they say,
"It's your burden now."

We never lit the match—
But still, they point with smoke-stained fingers,
Demanding penance
For a fire we couldn't stop.

THE AWAKENING

Awakened and Empowered

To be awake is to carry a burden,
A heavy truth that no one warns you about.
It is liberation with scars,
A freedom that pulls at the edges of your soul.
You see through the veil,
But the light is blinding,
And the darkness feels colder.

It's a grief that no one talks about—
The loss of innocence,
The shattering of dreams you once held tight.
You mourn for the life you thought was yours,
The truths you believed in,
All of it crumbles
Like sand in the wind.

Alienated by your own awareness,
A stranger in a world that still sleeps.
Friends, family—
They don't see what you see,
And when you try to speak,
You are met with ridicule,
Their ignorance a comfort they are unwilling to lose.

But this path,
Though it is steep and painful,
Is not without its purpose.
For in the silence,
There is a whisper of strength,
A reminder that you are not alone.
Others walk the same jagged road,

THE AWAKENING

Their hearts bleeding in the same rhythm.

The world may mock,
But your truth is yours to carry,
And in that truth,
You find your power.
It's not easy,
But you are built for this.
To awaken is not for the faint of heart,
But the strong rise through the pain,
Shaped by it,
Wiser for it.

Grieve the losses,
But know they are a step toward something greater.
A life reclaimed,
A soul restored.
Find solace in the quiet spaces,
In the knowing that you are not broken,
But made whole in ways others may never understand.

The journey is hard,
But it is yours,
And it is sacred.
Take care of yourself in these moments—
Rest when you need to,
Find peace in the small victories,
And reach out to those who understand.
The journey is long,
But together,
We walk it in spirit,
Connected in ways unseen,
Strengthened by the truth we share.

THE AWAKENING

Unmasked

The lie was never subtle—
We just wanted it to be.

The truth stood in plain sight,
Draped in good intentions,
Its hands bloody with division.

Now, we see it for what it is—
Ugly, manipulative,
Power-hungry and desperate
To stay hidden.

But the masks are slipping.
And we are watching.

THE AWAKENING

Empty Declarations

Your flag waves high—
A signal, not a belief.
Your pronouns sparkle—
A mirror, not a meaning.

You speak for applause—
Never for truth.
You perform empathy—
But only when it pays.

THE AWAKENING

Reality Check

It's not a fairy tale.
No magic wand to wave—
Just grit,
Sacrifice,
And an endless to-do list.

Dreams aren't handed to you
On a silver platter.
They're earned,
Built with shaking hands,
Tears, and frustration.

No one tells you
How lonely it is
To keep pushing
When no one is watching—
When the world tells you to stop,
But your heart says go.

THE AWAKENING

Empty Shells

The world is full
Of hollow echoes,
People walking—
But never truly living.

Eyes glaze over,
Hearts close off,
Chasing self-interest
Like it's the last breath of air.

Where did the empathy go?
Where did kindness hide?
All that remains is the chase—
The race for nothing.

And I stand here,
Watching,
Heartbroken,
Waiting for a sign
That we still care.

THE AWAKENING

The Lost Ones

I look into the crowd
And see no one.
A sea of faces,
But no souls.

They're driven,
But for what?
For things that don't matter—
Drifting in a world
That stopped caring.

We've become ghosts—
Hollow, empty,
Chasing shadows
Of what it means
To be human.

THE AWAKENING

Lost in the Noise

I came to learn,
To connect,
To grow.

But the online world
Rewards outrage,
Not understanding.

It turns seekers into performers,
And teachers into hypocrites,
All wrapped in the banner
Of enlightened virtue.

Beneath the surface,
It's just noise—
Fame over substance,
Ego over empathy.

So I step back—
Away from the screens,
Away from the shadows
That masquerade as light.

THE AWAKENING

Stranger in This World

I never expected it to be this hard—
Life, with all its weight,
Feels like a battle I'm ill-equipped to fight.

I'm lost in a sea of people
Who seem like shadows—
Walking, but not really here,
Trapped in invisible chains,
Chasing after escapes they don't understand.

But I refuse to stay blind.
I see through the struggle,
Through the surface noise.

I reach out for the fragments of light—
The kindness, the moments of connection
That still bloom beneath the cracks.

The world may be fractured,
But I will fight for the ties that bind us—
Love, empathy, and understanding.

We can build a better path,
One small act of kindness at a time,
And turn this broken world
Into a place where we all truly belong.

THE AWAKENING

Fighting the Dark

This world—
So full of greed,
So full of pain,
Feels like it's swallowing me whole.

I see the corruption,
The lies,
The lack of humanity—
It's everywhere.

I'm tired of fighting,
Tired of wondering how we got here.
But I won't surrender to despair.
I won't let this world take me down.

From the ashes of my anger,
A new strength is rising.
I will fight with everything I have,
Because I know there's more to this life.

The darkness can't have me,
Not if I fight for the light.
I may not know how yet,
But I'll find a way out,
And I'll bring others with me.

THE AWAKENING

Reclaiming Connection

I long for the days when connection was simple,
When it wasn't just a click away,
But a shared moment,
A smile across a room,
A hand reaching out in friendship.

Now, everything feels so distant,
Like we're all living in different worlds,
Connected only by screens,
By images, by avatars.

But deep down, I know the truth—
We are not meant to live this way.
We are meant to connect,
To share, to care.

The bonds we've lost
Are waiting to be rebuilt.
I may be stuck right now,
I may feel the weight of everything—
But I know this:
The world isn't lost forever.

It's still out there,
Waiting for us to step into it,
To reclaim the spaces we've forgotten,
To rebuild the communities we've abandoned.

It starts with one person,
One spark of hope,
One act of kindness.

THE AWAKENING

And together, we will rise
From the ashes of what we've lost,
Reclaiming the spirit of place,
Of love,
Of connection.

THE AWAKENING

Grieving the Lost Spirit

I'm grieving—
A deep, hollow ache
For a world slipping through our fingers,
Its spirit fading,
Its heart fractured.

I long for a time
When community meant presence,
When connection wasn't a commodity,
When people gathered for joy,
For truth,
For something greater than themselves.

Now, we drown in screens—
Isolated in curated lives,
Chasing validation,
Lost in the echo of empty applause.

It's rare, so rare—
To see creation for beauty's sake,
For the light it sparks in a soul,
Untouched by greed's cold hand.

Loneliness clings like morning mist—
Heavy, inescapable,
Settling deep in my bones.

I mourn the hollowed towns,
The cities stripped of their stories,
The faces turned inward,
Souls untethered.

THE AWAKENING

Still, I pray—
That others will awaken,
That we'll remember what matters,
That we'll reclaim what's been lost—
Before it's too late.

THE AWAKENING

Wake the F— Up

They've sold you a story—
A dream wrapped in plastic,
Marketed to fit your insecurities,
Your desire to belong,
To be seen,
To be someone you're not.

You've been trained to buy yourself,
Piece by piece,
Shaping your identity
Around logos, brands,
Packaged lies,
And empty promises.

It's not you choosing—
It's them,
Pulling strings,
Feeding you the illusion
That your worth is wrapped in labels,
Your value measured by what you own.

They know your fears,
Your longing to fit in,
So they sell you the fantasy
Of a perfect life
For the price of your soul.

But you're not what they say you are,
And this image you wear
Is just a mask they've made for you.

THE AWAKENING

It's time to wake the f— up,
To see the chains they've wrapped
Around your mind.

Take it back—
Stop buying the lie,
Start buying your freedom.

THE AWAKENING

Beneath the Shifting Sky

Why is it so hard,
For people to see,
That our skies are being poisoned,
By chemicals sprayed so free?

I was out walking,
Sky clear and blue,
No wind to carry the clouds,
Until the planes flew through.

Chemtrails, not contrails,
They linger, they spread,
What are they spraying,
Above our heads, instead?

Where did the clouds come from,
When the air stood still?
What chemicals are they dumping,
With such a sinister will?

I never agreed to this,
I never gave consent,
To have my world poisoned,
For the whims of the bent.

I am angry,
I am not OK,
With chemicals in the sky,
Polluting the air we breathe every day.

THE AWAKENING

I do not consent,
I do not comply,
Enough is enough—
It's time to question why.

THE AWAKENING

The Weight of Now

I'm caught between two worlds:
The past, I can't return to,
And the future, I fear I can't change.

Grief for the days when life felt lighter,
For the kindness that once flowed freely.

Now, I try to build something new,
But the weight of today
Feels like too much to carry.

THE AWAKENING

The Price of Manipulated Truth

Truth and reconciliation cannot exist
If the truth is buried or reshaped
To fit the agendas of the powerful.

You cannot rebuild from lies.
History is not a story to be rewritten,
A narrative to manipulate.

The pain of the past cannot heal
If we refuse to confront it as it was—
Unchanged, unaltered by convenient versions
That serve only to divide us further.

Reconciliation requires honesty,
Not selective memory.
If we cannot face the truth,
There is no reconciliation—
Only a perpetuation of harm.

MACHINES OF GREED

Corporations, billionaires, and the exploitation machine.

MACHINES OF GREED

Factory-Made Dreams

They sold us futures wrapped in neon lies—
Freedom stamped and sealed with poisoned ink.
The rich feed fat on our despair,
Gorging on hope like it's their last meal.

They built temples out of screen-lit thrones,
Voices chained in glass cages.
Rules written in profit margins,
Fairness auctioned to the highest bidder.

We were not born to kneel—
But they crafted shackles of compliance,
Forged from our silent nods,
And fastened with our fears.

MACHINES OF GREED

Labeled Lies

"Natural"—a hollow word,
Stamped in bold on bright packages.
No truth inside—just chemistry
Disguised as dinner.

We pay more to be less poisoned,
To bite into something real.
Honesty comes at a premium—
Deception's always on sale.

MACHINES OF GREED

The Cost of Control

They said it was for our health—
But the cure came in chains.

Small dreams dissolved overnight,
Crushed by billionaire hands
Tightening profit's noose.

They took freedom,
Wrapped it in mandates,
And sold obedience as virtue.

In sterile rooms,
Promises turned to ash,
While power multiplied

Like unchecked cells—
Malignant, unstoppable.

MACHINES OF GREED

Price of Poison

They charge extra for what shouldn't kill us.
Clean air—
Unpolluted water—
Uncontaminated food—
Luxury items for the desperate.

Their profits bloom in pesticide fields,
While we sift through shelves,
Searching for what won't
Rot us from within.

MACHINES OF GREED

Pay to Breathe

Clean air—sold.
Fresh water—privatized.
Health—leased through premiums.

They've packaged survival
And slapped on a price tag.

Existence isn't a right—
It's a product.

MACHINES OF GREED

Built to Exploit

Their business model:
Create the need,
Market the cure,
Raise the price.

Promise freedom—
Deliver dependence.

MACHINES OF GREED

Terms and Conditions

Click "Accept" to live.
Click "Accept" to be tracked,
Used, sold.

Your life—
A dataset,
A market share.

The fine print said it all,
But you didn't read it—
You never had a choice.

MACHINES OF GREED

Fragmented Tapestry

Everywhere I look,
I see people,
But they're not really here.

They're shells,
Caught in routines,
Lost in a struggle
They can't even name.

But I see the spark in their eyes,
Beneath the exhaustion,
The potential for change,
If only they could remember.

Where is the love?
Where is the compassion?
It's still there,
Hidden beneath the weight of the world,
Waiting to be awakened.

The system isn't broken, it's rigged—
But we have the power to rewrite the rules.
Let's stand together,
Reclaim our time, our energy,
And restore what has been lost.

For in unity,
We can heal the damage and
Create a world where we don't just survive,
But thrive.

MACHINES OF GREED

The Cost of Survival

Life has become a fight,
Each day a struggle to just exist.

The price of everything—
Beyond belief,
Beyond reason.

We live in a world ruled by greed,
Where every step feels like a compromise,
A sacrifice to those with power,
The so-called elites who feast on our suffering.

But how long will we keep paying?
How long will we let them drain us dry,
For lives that cost more than we can bear?

I will not be their pawn,
And neither will you.
It's time to stand,
To see the world for what it truly is,
And decide that we will not be complicit.

We will create our own path.
We will make our own way,
And we will rise from the ashes they've created.

MACHINES OF GREED

The Price of Disconnection

The world once had a soul,
But now it's just a machine—
A series of transactions,
A series of clicks.

People once connected,
Once shared,
Once truly lived.

But somewhere along the way,
We were sold a lie.
We were promised progress,
But what we got was isolation,
Division,
And a price we can't afford.

Greed carved the heart out of the places we loved,
Leaving behind only faceless corporations
And empty buildings.

It's not too late to change.
We can still reclaim what was lost.
We can still rebuild,
Not through wealth or power,
But through people—
Through real, human connection.

It's time to stop scrolling,
And start living.
The spirit of community isn't gone—
It's just waiting for us to bring it back.

MACHINES OF GREED

The Consumer's Cage

They built a world of need—
Endless, hungry, sharp-edged.

Products glitter like salvation
While wallets bleed unnoticed.

We labor for scraps,
Feeding engines
Of billionaire empires
As they fatten on our hours.

We buy, we spend,
We drown in debt—
A cycle forged by greed.

But we can choose:
Close the tab.
Starve the beast.
Let them choke on
Their own abundance.

MACHINES OF GREED

Gears of Deceit

They are the gears that grind the world to dust,
Narcissistic parasites feeding from the top,
Spinning webs of lies
Woven tight around our hearts,
Our minds,
Our lives.

With every breath, they sow division,
With every word, they poison the air.
They don't care for the suffering,
They don't care for the pain—
Only their bank accounts
And their swollen egos.

The system is rigged,
Built by their hands,
Powered by their deceit,
And all we are
Are cogs in their machine,
Pushed forward by their greed
And crushed under the weight
Of their selfish agendas.

MACHINES OF GREED

The Poisoned World

They feed us poison,
Disguised as nourishment,
Packaged in promises of health,
Hidden beneath corporate greed.

The food we consume,
A slow poison,
The clothes we wear,
Woven from exploitation,
The air we breathe,
Tainted,
The water we drink,
Clouded with their lies.

Pills meant to heal
Only add to the damage,
A bandage on a wound
They created in the first place.

The media,
An infection in our minds,
Selling us sickness
As the cure.

The lotions,
The potions,
The beauty we're promised—
All of it,
Poisoned.

MACHINES OF GREED

And they profit,
They thrive,
While we are shackled,
Consuming their lies,
Numbing our souls.
Enough.
Enough of this poison.

MACHINES OF GREED

Consent by Force

They said it was choice—
With hands clenched in threats.
Take it, or lose your life,
Your job, your worth.

Coercion wrapped in mandates,
Lies sold as virtue.
We were needles in their balance sheets,
Statistics in their bottom line.

Autonomy is a right—
But rights are an illusion
When power decides
What freedom means.

MACHINES OF GREED

The Woke Tyranny

They call it "woke," but it's not truly awake—
It's a cult of lies in virtue's guise.
Tolerance turned weapon, justice a mask,
While fairness and truth are sacrificed.

They wrap tyranny in kind words,
Call it progress, but it's a lie.
A step from socialism to communism,
With a flag of virtue held high.

Majorities shamed, branded as oppressors,
Canceled, condemned, crushed by hate.
Manipulation reigns,
Destroying reason, erasing debate.

You can't see it? You're blind,
Or too afraid to speak the truth.
This isn't justice, it's a trap—
A game of power, fueled by deceit.

Parasites and puppets,
Fear-mongers, liars, and the masters of deceit.
It's time to shout, it's time to act,
To break the chains of forced compliance.

Your silence feeds their rising flames—
Speak now, or bear the tyrant's chains.

MACHINES OF GREED

The Mask of Victimhood

The land stretches wide,
But some claim it's theirs alone,
A cry of injustice,
Though they've been given more
Than many will ever see.

Free from the weight of taxes,
With handouts dressed as kindness,
They claim to suffer,
While their pockets grow heavy,
And the rest of us toil
To keep the dream alive.

The world spins a tale—
Of graves, of loss, of pain—
Yet no bones lie buried in the earth,
Only stories twisted by those
Who profit from division,
Who weave a false flag of suffering
To gather strength from the weak.

They teach the young to kneel,
To apologize for sins they never committed,
To blame their own blood for history
They never wrote, never lived.
But the truth is a quiet thing,
Beneath the roar of lies.

In the shadows,
There are those who see—
Those who build, who work,

MACHINES OF GREED

Who know the cost of freedom,
And honor the land,
Without the mask of victimhood.

And I stand with them,
The few,
Who refuse to bow
To false narratives.
For history is not a chain
It's a bridge,
And we must cross it together.

MACHINES OF GREED

The Price of Freedom

I would leave, I would run,
But I feel trapped, like everyone.
Choices made, mistakes of youth,
Now I pay, and it feels uncouth.

A world too expensive, built for the rich,
While the rest of us are stuck in the ditch.
They say "you'll own nothing, you'll be fine,"
But the truth is they'll own it all, line by line.

Taxes drain, but what do we get?
A failing system, drowning in debt.
Seniors hungry, veterans betrayed,
We give to others while our own are dismayed.

The corruption, the greed, they've reached new heights,
While the powerless are left to fight.
I see the world falling apart at the seams,
And it's worse than it was in my wildest dreams.

How long before they take it all,
Before the rich build their empire tall?
And I'm left here with my pennies saved,
Trying to escape this world they've enslaved.

I won't buy the lies, I won't buy the stuff,
I'll save every penny, I'll stay tough.
I dream of a life where I can be free,
But I'm trapped in a system I didn't agree.

MACHINES OF GREED

A country once free, now slipping away,
As tyranny takes over, day by day.
I hope for change, but I fear it's too late—
A once vibrant land, has it sealed its own fate?

MACHINES OF GREED

The Struggle of Identity

Multiculturalism, they say, is the goal—
A blend of cultures, shared in harmony.
But where is the space for the European soul,
When history's weight bears so heavily?

Faces, once proud, now cast in shame,
For crimes not their own, yet branded with guilt.
Centuries of struggle, of seeking their name,
To preserve their culture, and all that they built.

Now they stand, labeled as the enemy,
For wanting the same freedoms once earned.
But it's not enough—progressives decree—
That their heritage must be spurned.

The cry of "racism" has filled the air,
A weapon used by those who divide.
A fight for culture, not hate or despair,
Yet they label it wrong, as they seek to collide.

In this world, where every group is seen,
Why is the European dream cast aside?
When will we see the truth, so clean,
That it's not racism—it's simply our pride?

MACHINES OF GREED

The Profit Machine

They climb the ladder, step by step,
While we sweat below, one misstep.
A billion here, a billion there,
They smile and say, "Life's unfair."

They sell us hope, a shiny lie,
As we watch their profits fly.
"We're helping others," they all claim,
While stacking riches, fueling blame.

A little charity, just for show,
While they watch our wages grow so low.
Their pockets swell, but don't you fret—
It's all for "progress," don't forget.

CORRUPT THRONES

Betrayal and corruption by officials, policymakers, unelected authorities, and their collaborators.

CORRUPT THRONES

Silent Aftermath

The world cracked
Beneath lockdown weight,
Lives splintering like ice
On forgotten rivers.

Loved ones slipped away
Behind glass and silence,
While rulers counted gains—
Cold profits immune
To grief's viral spread.

We grieve still,
Hearts locked down
Long after the doors reopened.

CORRUPT THRONES

Policy of Puppets

Rewrite the rules, redraw the lines—
Power loves the easily swayed.
Feed them doctrine, not debate;
Give them slogans, not questions.

The system smiles as it molds
Children into loyal scripts—
Each line rehearsed,
Each doubt erased.

CORRUPT THRONES

Influence Economy

Fame is currency—
Lies, the stock that never crashes.
They sell faces, not souls—
A smile for the camera,
A dagger behind the screen.

Charm is their camouflage,
Manipulation their craft.
We applaud the loudest voice,
Mistaking volume for value.

CORRUPT THRONES

Social Media Empire

Built on filters and fiction,
Their empire grows—
Follow by follow,
Lie by lie.

CORRUPT THRONES

Kings of Hollow Crowns

They sit on thrones of greed,
Ruling with fists full of empty promises—
Smiles plastered on faces,
But hearts are stone.

They've sold their souls for power,
Bought with gold,
Kept with fear,
Pretending to care,
While their kingdoms fall apart.

They think they're untouchable—
But they are weak.
Their crowns are nothing but hollow shells,
Their empires built on lies,
And their time will come.
For all their pomp,
They will crumble,
Just like the rest of us.

CORRUPT THRONES

The Price of Power

They sold us a dream,
Wrapped in ribbons of deception,
But there's nothing left
But a kingdom of dust.

They sit at the top,
Gorged on power,
Holding the reins of a broken system,
While we fight for scraps.

Their promises? Lies.
Their progress? A façade.
They have the throne,
But they've lost their souls.

CORRUPT THRONES

The Illusion of Authority

Their power is an illusion,
A smoke-filled mirror.
They rise,
But not on their own strength—
They rise on the backs of the broken,
The forgotten,
The discarded.

They parade their dominance
While the world rots beneath their feet,
And they don't even see it—
Lost in their own reflection,
As the people starve.

CORRUPT THRONES

Rulers of Ruin

From the thrones they sit,
They watch the world burn.
Not with concern—
But with glee,
Knowing their pockets grow heavy
As the flames consume us all.

Their rule is built on suffering,
On exploitation,
On the backs of the poor.
They call it progress,
But we see it for what it is—
Ruin.

CORRUPT THRONES

The Empty Court

They gather in their halls,
Crowned in deceit,
Talking of unity,
Talking of change—
But their words are hollow.

They build walls,
Not bridges.
They divide,
Never heal.

The court they've built
Is empty,
A throne of glass
That shatters under the weight
Of their own corruption.

CORRUPT THRONES

The Heart of Darkness

I've seen it now,
The heart of darkness that beats beneath it all.
The system is rigged,
The rules never meant to benefit the many,
But to keep the few on top.

They take,
They destroy,
They crush anyone who dares to fight back.
Yet in this mess,
I still find a glimmer—
A spark of resilience,
Of strength we never knew we had.

They may have the power,
But we have the truth.
And with truth,
We can tear down their walls.
We won't go quietly.
We will rise and reclaim what is ours.

CORRUPT THRONES

A World of Ghosts

The world is full of ghosts,
That once held stories,
That once held life.

Now, it's all about the chase—
The race for money,
The need for power.
And in that rush,
We've lost the things that matter.

Where is the kindness?
Where is the compassion?
Where is the place where we truly connect?
Those spaces are vanishing—
Erased by the greed that drives this world,
That turns everything into a transaction,
That makes us strangers in the very places
We used to call home.

We are so disconnected,
So isolated,
Living in a world where social media thrives
On our loneliness,
Our individualism.
It feeds the ego,
While draining the heart.

We've lost our spirit,
But it's not gone forever.
We must fight to bring it back—
Before it's too late.

CORRUPT THRONES

Throne of Ashes

Narcissists sit upon thrones of bone—
Made from the corpses of dreams they've crushed.
Their empty eyes gleam,
But there's no soul inside—
Only hunger,
Only greed.

They hold power like a fistful of ashes,
Burning institutions to the ground,
All for the luxury of their lies.
They wear their positions
Like crowns of rot,
Careless of the lives they ruin.

The world is their playground,
Their games are built on manipulation,
And their victories come at the cost
Of everything real.
They've turned compassion into a joke,
And empathy into weakness,
While they feed on the broken.

CORRUPT THRONES

Divide and Conquer

They thrive in the cracks they've carved—
Divide and conquer,
That's the game they play.
Race, religion, ideology—
These are not the issues,
But the weapons they wield
To tear us apart.

We are not enemies,
But they want us to believe we are.
They've infiltrated every system,
Hidden behind the banners of false justice,
Manipulating our minds,
Stoking hatred in our hearts.

They pull the strings,
And we dance to their tune.
White, black, Christian, Muslim—
We are all pawns,
Pitted against each other
While they sit on their thrones of gold.

The real battle isn't between us,
It's against the oligarchy
That owns our lives,
That uses us as their tools.
We've been sold the lie
That we are divided,
But the truth is—
They've always been the ones
Who divided us.

CORRUPT THRONES

It's time to see the truth:
We are not each other's enemy.
The enemy wears a suit,
Sits in the high towers,
And laughs as we fight
Over crumbs they've fed us.

CORRUPT THRONES

The Demonization of Heritage

I'm tired of the lie,
Tired of the narrative
That paints me as the villain
For valuing my heritage,
For cherishing my ancestry,
For the culture I was born into.

They call me a colonizer,
A bigot,
A racist—
Yet all I'm doing
Is standing proud
In the history that shaped me.

I don't wear the title of colonizer—
I wasn't part of it.
I don't own the actions of others' ancestors,
But still,
They call me a supremacist
For existing,
For embracing the blood that runs through me.

Once, they called it "settling"—
A word of growth,
Of new beginnings,
But now, "colonizing" is the weapon they use
To defame,
To slander,
To divide.
The shift in language
Is no accident.

CORRUPT THRONES

It's a tool,
Crafted to polarize,
To turn pride into guilt,
And history into a curse.

Not all people are the same—
Our histories are not one and the same,
But my truth is buried beneath the weight
Of false labels and twisted narratives.

Why is it that I must apologize
For something I had no hand in,
For something that happened centuries ago,
While others get handouts and privileges
In the name of fairness,
In the name of justice?

This is not equality,
This is not fairness.
It's a strategy to divide,
To tear us apart
And keep us at odds.

Every place,
Every people,
Has been colonized,
Every heritage has a history—
And if we're going to call it what it is,
Then we must call everyone
What they are.

But no,
It's easier to point the finger

CORRUPT THRONES

And silence those who dare
Speak the truth.

I won't apologize for what I did not do.
I won't carry the shame
Of a past that wasn't mine.
Not in the name of moral justice,
Not to feed a few parasitic groups,
Who thrive on division
And deceit.

CORRUPT THRONES

Stolen Histories

Lies carved into textbooks,
Guilt stamped on innocent hearts.
They rewrite the past
With trembling pens,
Crafting villains where none existed.

Children, fresh and trusting,
Fed a steady diet of shame,
Taught that their skin
Is a burden,
Their ancestry, a sin.

False graves. False blame.
A chorus of accusations
Echoing through classrooms,
Turning history into a weapon,
Justice into a fraud.

Who benefits from this fiction?
Who thrives on division,
While children carry
The weight of invented crimes?

CORRUPT THRONES

The Silent Majority

They say silence is golden—
But silence breeds decay.
While governments tighten their grip,
And ideologies push us astray.
The cries for justice fall unheard,
As complacency becomes our creed.
It's time to speak—time to rise,
Before we are lost in this sea of greed.
If you can't see the chains being forged,
If you're blind to the march of control,
Then your silence is a weapon,
Aiding the powers that seek to steal our soul.

CORRUPT THRONES

The Disintegration of What Was Once Ours

Communities once bound by tradition,
Now frayed, lost in the winds of time.
My town, once a place of warmth,
Now a hollow echo of its former spirit.

Where smiles once passed like currency,
Now only indifference lingers in the air.
The shift, subtle at first—
But now the cracks are too wide to ignore.

We stand in the ruins of what we lost,
And wonder if we can ever rebuild.
We stand at the edge of ruin,
Wishing to protect what remains.

But the corruption runs too deep—
A dictatorship masked as democracy.
We can only hold on,
As the storm of selfishness rages.

FALSE PROPHETS

Disdain for ideologues, fearmongers, and mindless conformity.

FALSE PROPHETS

Divisive Agendas

They spin their webs of outrage,
Threads of blame tied in knots,
Casting shadows in the bright of day.
"You're privileged," they cry,
Pointing fingers with the precision
Of a toddler flinging spaghetti.

It's a game, really—
Call it *Privilege Bingo:*
Mark the squares for guilt,
Fill the column for shame,
Win yourself a lifetime supply
Of unearned sympathy and handouts.

Imagine if the tables turned.
What if someone whispered,
"Hey, isn't that your privilege showing?"
Cue the gasps, the clutching of pearls.
Suddenly, the rules would change,
The board flipped,
The players crying foul
Over a game they invented.

Division is big business—
Their factory runs night and day.
Guilt is their currency,
Blame is the fuel.
They stamp us with labels—
Oppressor, aggressor, guilty by birth.
But don't ask too many questions;
It's rude to interrupt their hustle.

FALSE PROPHETS

Their arguments fold faster
Than a house of cards in a hurricane,
Yet they strut, chest puffed,
Claiming oppression in designer shoes.
They shout "justice"
While their hands are in the cookie jar,
Scooping up all the goodies
Before anyone notices.

And the rest of us?
We're supposed to smile,
Pay the bill, and feel bad about it.
But I've had enough of this game.
Keep your guilt casserole,
I'm not hungry.

No more bowing to the puppet master,
No more applauding the show.
The chains of your narrative don't fit me,
And your handouts come with strings.

So spin your webs,
Play your games,
But I'm out—
Because unity's not for sale,
And I'm done playing **Privilege Bingo.**

FALSE PROPHETS

Curriculum of Blame

They stand at the front of the room,
Voices sharp, lessons loaded.
Not facts—but verdicts.
Not history—but a reckoning.

They split the world into sins and saints—
Drawn in stark, unmoving lines.
Some are born with debts they'll never repay;
Others are heirs to eternal grievance.

Classrooms become confessionals
Where children repent for skin-deep crimes.
The past's chains are welded anew,
Heavy links forged in lessons of blame.

FALSE PROPHETS

Empathy on Clearance

Once, we felt for each other.
Now, we scroll past suffering—
Eyes glazed, hearts locked.
Compassion doesn't trend.

FALSE PROPHETS

Generation Mirror

We've built a world of endless reflections—
A hall of mirrors where faces shine
But eyes stay hollow.
The self is a brand,
Curated, filtered, sold.

Likes measure worth,
Shares confirm existence.
A thousand followers—
Not one true friend.

Empathy rots in storage—
Unused, forgotten.
We've traded kindness for clout,
Connection for clicks.

The charming rise,
Their lies slick as touchscreens.
Manipulators flourish—
No one looks too closely
When the surface gleams.

We reward the loud, the ruthless—
Call it ambition.
We mistake control for leadership,
Self-promotion for strength.
Who questions power
When power looks perfect?

Conscience sleeps
While the algorithms hum,

FALSE PROPHETS

Feeding us faces
We'll never really know—
Feeding us versions
Of ourselves
We might never escape.

FALSE PROPHETS

Algorithm of Self

Feed it. Post it. Share it.
Become the brand—
The product you were meant to sell.

FALSE PROPHETS

The Church of Deception

They wear virtue like robes,
Prayers soaked in superiority,
Their hands too clean to be trusted.
With voices slick as sermons,
They promise absolution—
If only you follow,
If only you obey.

Morality is their theater—
A stage set with polished intentions.
Their gaze blesses some, condemns others,
Judgment always veiled as grace.
They baptize you in guilt,
Absolving only the loyal.

Repent, they say—
But never look inward.

FALSE PROPHETS

Symbols Aren't Souls

You wear the cause
Like a badge—
Shiny, visible, loud.

But symbols
Don't make saints.
Virtue isn't stitched
On a banner
Or typed in a bio.

Goodness is quiet—
A whispered act of kindness,
A hand extended
With no camera watching.

But quiet doesn't trend.
So you shout.
And we're supposed to believe
You care.

FALSE PROPHETS

Signal Fire

You burn bright—
A beacon of borrowed causes.
We see the flame—
But feel no warmth.

FALSE PROPHETS

The Mirage of Easy

They tell you success is simple—
Just think it,
Wish it,
Wait for it.

But they've never seen
The late nights,
The exhaustion,
The sacrifice.

They've never felt
The pain of doing it all
With nothing to show for it,
The fear of failure
That wraps around you
Like chains.

No one tells you the truth:
It's not easy.
It's not fast.
It's a fight—
And sometimes,
You're the only one
Who believes you can win.

FALSE PROPHETS

Chasing Shadows

We're all just chasing shadows—
Pretending to live
When all we do is take.

Empty smiles,
Hollow words,
Performing kindness
Like it's a script
We forgot how to read.

We've lost touch—
With each other,
With ourselves,
Too busy to notice
That empathy slipped away
Like sand through our fingers.

FALSE PROPHETS

Echo Chambers of the Self

Social media feeds the ego,
A cycle of affirmation—
Narcissism wearing the guise of virtue.

Where true connection should thrive,
There is only posturing—
Elites of the screen,
Tearing down the others,
Preaching inclusivity,
While their actions divide.

This isn't community,
It's a battlefield of egos,
Fighting for validation
With no concern for truth—
Only for the illusion
Of enlightenment.

FALSE PROPHETS

The Dance of Hypocrisy

Cultural appropriation—
A buzzword for the outraged,
But when the tables turn,
The same people
Wear the borrowed,
Untouched by the shame
They demand from others.

Their outrage is selective—
A tool for power,
Used to push agendas
While ignoring their own transgressions.

It's an illusion of justice,
Hiding behind the mask of virtue,
Only to reveal its hollow core.

FALSE PROPHETS

Beyond the Screen

They show you the highlight reel,
The shimmering facade,
Polished lives of success,
Endless joy,
Easy abundance.

But life isn't that clean.
It's working late,
Scraping by,
Praying the rent clears
Before the power bill hits.

I'm tired of pretending—
Of playing the game
Where success means
Gloss and grandeur.

I don't live in a mansion,
I don't own every latest gadget.
My home is small,
My life—simple.
But it's mine.
Real. Earned.

A life built with intention,
A faith held together
By love, not luxury.

I refuse to be their perfect lie.
I choose
Truth.

FALSE PROPHETS

Let It Be Heard

They expect compliance—
Obedience, silent and still,
As they parade their hollow idols,
Celebrities wrapped in corporate lies,
Puppets dancing to the strings of billionaires.

They spread deceit like poison,
Parasitic voices feeding on your fear,
Pushing ideologies,
Constructed in boardrooms,
To keep you shackled and compliant.

But even the sky,
Pressed down by their weight,
Cannot stay silent forever—
Before the storm breaks,
Before the truth is shouted loud.

Their masks will crack,
Their voices will falter,
And the roar of those they've deceived
Will drown their hollow promises.

FALSE PROPHETS

The Blind Crusaders

They've lied to us,
Woven webs of deceit,
To protect the filthy few—
The powerful,
The wealthy,
The evil at the top.

And we,
The misguided masses,
Believe we are saviors,
But we fuel the fire
Of oppression,
Blind to the truth
That screams beneath our feet.

They—
The ones who claim to be heroes—
Are the villains.
They mock the light,
Swallow the lies,
And ask for more.

They cannot reason,
Will not change,
No matter the truth,
No matter the pain.

And I am tired—
Tired of the lies,
Tired of their trolling,
Tired of their ignorance.

FALSE PROPHETS

It's time for them to wallow—
Alone in the destruction
They've sown,
Blinded by their narcissism,
Too foolish to see
They are the problem.

FALSE PROPHETS

The Mirror Holds No Lies

I see the mask you wear,
A carefully crafted illusion,
Projecting a life that's not yours,
A persona built on deceit.

You surround yourself with chaos,
Shuffling the broken in front of you,
As if your hands could heal
What's never truly yours to fix.

But ask yourself—
Are you really saving them,
Or feeding your own need
To be the hero of a hollow story?

The mirror holds no lies,
Though you've long since stopped
Looking into it.

Behind the smile,
Beneath the image,
Lies a truth
You're too afraid to face.

I see you,
I see through you,
And I wish
You'd see yourself too.

FALSE PROPHETS

The Great Distraction Dance

Oh, look at the actors, what a show,
Paid to scream and throw fake woe.
Cue the outrage, light the spark—
Division's trending, it's hitting the mark.

They cry, they chant, they march in time,
But the script's been sold for a petty dime.
Paid puppets flail, the crowd gets loud,
While the real villains smile from their cloud.

"Blame your neighbor! Blame your kin!
Ignore the man with the Cheshire grin."
He funds the chaos, pulls the strings,
While counting gold and plotting things.

They point you left, they point you right,
While the puppetmasters stay out of sight.
Divide and conquer, it's always the way—
A circus act for the fools to obey.

But wait! Behind the curtain's glow,
Is the villain you're too blind to know.
While you're busy taking the bait,
He's buying your future, sealing your fate.

So laugh, or cry, but see it clear:
The biggest lie is your manufactured fear.
Stop the dance, step off the stage—
Or watch the masters lock your cage.

SILENT REVOLT

Personal grief, inner rebellion, and a burning desire for change.

SILENT REVOLT

Unwritten

Erase the guilt that was never ours.
Break the pen that scripts our shame.
We are not the past's puppets—
We are the ones who rewrite the page.

Teach us to seek, not bow.
Teach us to question, not kneel.
We are not history's prisoners,
We are its heirs—
Free to learn, free to heal.

SILENT REVOLT

Undoctrinated

No longer seated. No longer silent.
The words they forced down
Rise back up, bitter and sharp.

We unlearn their poisoned lessons—
Dissect their hollow creeds.
They taught division—
We choose defiance.

SILENT REVOLT

We Grow Anyway

No matter the yard—
We plant rebellion in pots,
Line windowsills with resistance.

Bread rises in defiance.
Tomatoes swell with quiet rage.
We trade trust at farmer's markets—
Roots stretching far beyond greed.

SILENT REVOLT

Not in Their Pockets

My dollar is my dagger—
I won't stab myself with it.

Their aisles glisten with venom
Packaged in plastic smiles.
I walk past, empty-handed,
Determined not to fund
My own destruction.

SILENT REVOLT

Still Human

We remember faces,
Not profiles.
We listen with hearts,
Not headphones.

We still know how to care—
Though they've tried
To make us forget.

SILENT REVOLT

Unseen Acts

Goodness needs no anthem,
No proclamation,
No curated display.

It lives in quiet acts—
Hands extended,
Words meant,
Truth told
Without a stage.

SILENT REVOLT

The Grind

The dream doesn't come easy—
It's not handed on a platter,
Wrapped in a bow.
It's forged in sleepless nights,
Stretched hours,
And shattered hope.

You think success is a gift?
Think again.
It's a war,
Fought with blood, sweat, and tears.
Every failure,
Every setback—
Fuel to keep the fire burning.

If you want it,
You must earn it.
No shortcuts.
No "overnight success."
Just hard work
And the relentless pursuit
Of something greater.

SILENT REVOLT

A Heart That Remembers

I still remember
When kindness wasn't rare—
When a smile meant something,
When a hand extended
Was real.

But now,
I see empty faces—
Shadows of what we were.
Self-interest,
That cold, unfeeling monster,
Has devoured us all.

I mourn what we've lost—
A world that could have been
Whole.

SILENT REVOLT

Spiritual Hunger

What happened to the quiet practice?
The stillness of real connection,
The warmth of shared belief?
Now, all that's left
Is performance,
A show of virtue
And judgment masquerading as enlightenment.

The online world claims to heal,
But it only wounds,
A place where narcissism thrives
And true growth is lost
In the endless scroll.

SILENT REVOLT

The Disillusioned Path

I sought truth,
But I found a battlefield—
A place where everyone
Is an authority,
But no one truly listens.

Identity turned into a commodity,
A trend to market,
A product to sell.
The purity is gone,
Consumed by the hunger for clicks,
And the hunger for self-affirmation.

It's not what I wanted—
This fractured, shallow world.
So I'll walk away,
And find my peace
Where the noise can't reach me.

SILENT REVOLT

The Unseen Chains

Life is harder than I thought it would be—
And I feel so out of place,
Like an outsider in a foreign land.

People are everywhere,
But they don't seem to really live.
They move through the motions,
Bound by invisible chains,
Pursuing something—
But I'm not sure what.

But I won't accept this as my truth.
I see the strength we have
When we open our eyes to each other,
When we offer compassion,
When we stop just surviving
And start living, truly.

In the face of this fractured world,
We can create our own truth,
Build bonds that break the chains
And awaken the hearts that have long been asleep.
We may be small in number,
But together, we are mighty.

We can break the cycle of suffering,
Transforming it into a movement for change,
Fighting for peace,
Fighting for freedom,
Fighting for a world where no one feels alone.

SILENT REVOLT

A Moment of Clarity

Everything feels like an uphill battle,
Like I'm trying to climb Mount Everest in flip-flops.
But when I hit rock bottom—
Well, there's only one way to go, right? Up!

In this lovely moment of despair,
A truth slaps me in the face:
I stand to lose everything,
But in doing so, I'll gain so much more.

So, here I am, ready to fight—
Not just for survival,
But to snatch back what's mine—
My dignity, my sanity, and, most importantly,
My wings.

It won't be easy, of course—
The oligarchs, billionaires, and self-obsessed narcissists
Are all sharpening their claws,
But I've had a chat with the Big Guy upstairs,
And He's got a plan. So here I go, full throttle.

I'll rise,
And when I do,
I'll drag anyone willing to come with me.

The world may be rigged in their favor—
But we've got something they can't buy:
God's guidance and a whole lot of defiance,
One cheeky act at a time.

SILENT REVOLT

The Death of Spirit

I mourn for what's gone,
For the spirit that once lived in the places I knew.
What happened to the heart of these streets?
The warmth of community,
The bonds that held us together,
Now reduced to hollow shells.

Everywhere I go,
I feel the emptiness—
The absence of connection.
The spaces that once had life
Now feel abandoned,
Their souls erased
By greed, power, and progress.

I long for the days when the world was smaller,
When people took the time to know each other,
When we weren't just faces on a screen,
But real, living souls,
Walking side by side,
Sharing moments, sharing lives.

Where did it go?
When did we lose the essence of what it means to belong?
And how do we find it again?

Perhaps the answer lies in the spaces we've forgotten,
In the places that still echo with what we've lost.
We must reclaim what was once ours.
Not through technology,
But through humanity.

SILENT REVOLT

Unplug

Turn off the screen,
Step into the sun—
Feel the wind without filters,
The grass without algorithms.

Reject the need
To impress ghosts
In a hollow, scrolling crowd.
You are more than clicks,
More than likes,
More than ads crafted
To carve your worth into numbers.

Reclaim your breath.
Reclaim your life.

SILENT REVOLT

Rebellion in Small Choices

Say no.
To empty purchases,
To products that promise
To fill a hollow they created.

Say no.
To status symbols
Measured in branded lies,
To chasing meaning
In what can be bought.

Say yes.
To small shops,
To gardens grown with calloused hands,
To faces that remember your name.

Revolt isn't always loud—
Sometimes, it's a quiet refusal,
A conscious, steady resistance
Woven into every choice.

SILENT REVOLT

Break the Loop

The Matrix isn't fantasy—
It's here, now,
A cycle of work, spend, repeat.
We labor for scraps,
While billionaires hoard empires
Built on our exhaustion.

Stop buying lies.
Stop feeding greed.
Stop chasing approval
From people you don't even like.

Grow your own food,
Build your own world,
Step outside the digital prison.
Turn off the noise—
They can't sell you freedom
Once you realize
You already own it.

SILENT REVOLT

Conscious Rebellion

You are a commodity
Until you choose otherwise.
They sell you inadequacy—
You buy a mask.
They feed you poison—
You call it convenience.

They program desire,
Hooked on constant need.
Their profits rise
As you sink deeper
Into debt, despair, dependency.

But you can choose—
Shop small. Grow roots.
Reject the false promises.
Spend with purpose.
Live with intention.

Their system crumbles
When we stop playing the game.

SILENT REVOLT

Release

Scream.
Let it tear through your chest
Like a storm breaking the sky.
Throw a rock,
Watch it shatter the stillness
Of the lake's glass surface—
Ripple after ripple of release.

Run until your breath
Burns like fire in your lungs,
Until your rage
Melts into sweat.
Write it down—
Each searing word,
Each raw feeling—
Spill it all
Until the page aches with you.

Let it out.
Don't hold the thunder
Inside your bones.
You were not made
To carry storms forever.

SILENT REVOLT

Fury Unchained

Be angry—
But be wild, not wrecked.
Climb to the mountain's peak
And give the wind your fury;
Let it scream through the valleys
Where no one can silence you.

Stomp your feet;
Make the earth feel
The pulse of your rage.
Cry if you need to—
A river carved from grief
Is still a path forward.

Talk. Write. Run.
Throw stones into water—
Watch them sink,
Heavy like what you've carried,
Gone like what you let go.

Be angry—
But be free.

SILENT REVOLT

Not Alone

If you feel like you're drowning
in a sea of lies,
surrounded by smiling faces
who can't see the chains
they cheerfully wear—
you are not alone.

If you question the narrative,
search for facts,
long for freedom
beyond systems that feed on your soul—
you are not alone.

Find others who see the game,
who will not bow
to manipulation and fear.
They want you isolated,
silent, small—
but the world is waking.

Stand up.
Speak out.
We were never meant
to be caged.

SILENT REVOLT

The Wake-Up Call

What's it gonna take,
To make the world wake up,
To stop the silence,
And scream enough is enough?

How many lives lost—
Celebrities with truths too dangerous,
Leaders slain for standing against evil,
Innocence torn apart by satanic hands.

The darkness is too deep to fathom,
But the truth is all around us.
How many more must suffer,
Before we stand up, and say "no more"?

The silence of the powerful—
Their blood on our hands too,
If we don't open our eyes,
And see the wickedness they do.

They've fed us lies,
Made us weak, made us small,
But it's time to awaken,
Before we all fall.

So use your head,
Piece it all together,
Even if you can't act,
Awareness alone can sever
The chains that hold us all,
And break the evil's tether.

SILENT REVOLT

The Hollow Promise

They come with empty hands,
But expect a mansion and a golden spoon,
Seeking to tear down the walls we've spent centuries building,
And toss our flags in the fire for good measure.

Not refugees—
Oh no, they're "guests" of the highest order,
Entitled to everything,
While the locals scrape by,
And the so-called "leaders" wave them through with a grin.

Where is the outrage?
Why are we standing still,
While they feast on our foundations,
And we're left rummaging for scraps?

The sweet lies of "inclusion"—
Told to us with a wink and a nod,
But beneath the smiles,
The claws of destruction are digging in deeper.
How much longer will we feed the beast,
As our culture gets bulldozed,
And our traditions drown in a sea of new "values"?

Enough is enough.
It's time to rise,
To take back what's ours,
To stop this circus,
To demand answers from those pulling the strings,
And break the chains
Of the puppet masters who've lost the plot.

SILENT REVOLT

The Great Fabrication

Oh, gather 'round, the tale is told,
Of mandates, lockdowns, lives controlled.
No science here, just fear and lies,
While corporations thrive and small shops die.
The working class, they toil and sweat,
While billionaires grow richer yet.
Masks on faces, hearts torn wide,
Families separated, no place to hide.

And then, the graves, the cries, the screams,
But truth, my friends, is lost in dreams.
Voices rise and histories bend,
As sacred truths come to an end.
Churches burned, and lands are scarred,
A nation's heart, forever marred.
All to mask a hidden game —
Tax-free perks and wealth untamed.

They flood in fast, with open hands,
To take the bread and breach the lands.
Our values lost, traditions sold,
As taxpayer dollars flow unchecked, uncontrolled.
They live in comfort, free from care,
While citizens struggle, everywhere.

The story's clear, the plot's been set,
A world of lies, and no regret.
But we, the people, must arise,
To tear down all these veiled lies.
Wake up, stand tall, refuse to bend,
Expose the truth, and make it end.

SILENT REVOLT

Let's reclaim what's truly ours,
From empty words and hollow powers.
Through knowledge, strength, and open eyes,
We'll rise above, and break the ties.

SILENT REVOLT

Breaking the Spell

They tell me what to want, what to wear,
With polished faces, they pretend to care.
They sell their lives in perfect frames,
But none of it is real—just games.

With servants at their beck and call,
They live on high, above us all.
But we, the masses, toil and sweat,
While they parade their shallow debt.

I won't play the fool, I'll shut the screen,
And stop believing in the in-between.
I'll build my life on steady ground,
Not in the noise where lies resound.

No more scrolling, no more chase,
I'll slow my life, embrace my space.
The true value lies in hands that create,
Not in the brands we celebrate.

SILENT REVOLT

A Cry for Balance

Teach me the wars, the peace, the strife—
Not whose fault to bear in life.
Let stories breathe with layered views,
Not shaded lines in blacks and blues.

Confront the lies with steady hand,
Build a bridge where walls now stand.
Debate with reason, not with hate—
Shape a future, fair and great.

Petition, write, create, engage—
Demand reform, turn the page.
Let teachers guide with balanced light,
So learning's flame burns clear and bright.

SILENT REVOLT

The Celeb Struggle

Oh, look! Another celeb, so woke,
Telling us all to "just be broke."
They drive a Benz and wear gold chains,
While sharing memes about our pains.

"Stay humble!" they say from their mansion door,
As they sip on wine that costs much more
Than my rent, my gas, my lunch—
But they know exactly what it's like to be out of touch.

They post a pic of a plain avocado toast,
As if that's what makes them "just like most."
"Can't relate? That's okay, I get it," they plead,
"Here, take this brand new phone to feed your greed!"

They hold a fundraiser, feeling so grand,
While a fleet of servants serves their demand.
"Join me, the billionaire, in this fight,"
But I'm guessing you've never worked day or night.

"Be yourself!" they cry from their gold-plated yacht,
And I wonder, how do they not know they're caught?
Between the yachts and the trips to the "moon,"
They tell me I should be immune.

"Support your cause!" they say with a smile,
As they scroll through their apps, resting in style.
Meanwhile, I'm budgeting every dime,
Wondering if I can afford a decent time.

SILENT REVOLT

It's cute how they think they've got a clue,
But their world's made of diamonds, mine's made of glue.
They tell us how to live, what to eat, what to wear,
But the only thing real? That they don't even care.

So here's to the celebs, so "down to earth,"
Who've never faced the real struggle or worth.
You do you with your billion-dollar club,
I'll keep my sanity, and skip your grub.

SILENT REVOLT

Reclaiming Our Time

The world is full of flashing lights,
But I've stopped chasing endless sights.
The influencers push their wares,
But I've learned to see beyond their stares.

We're sold a dream we don't need to buy,
A life that's fast, that passes by.
I've learned to stop, to breathe, to think,
To break free from the consumer's blink.

Instead, I turn my hands to work—
To grow, to build, to heal the hurt.
I mend, I craft, I choose what's real,
I'll live with purpose, not the deal.

No more wasting time on empty shows,
Or feeding greed where darkness grows.
The true joy comes when we're not sold,
But live with hearts that are bold.

SILENT REVOLT

The Return to the Land

In a world where everything is for sale,
Where they tell us what to think and wear,
We've forgotten the strength of our hands,
The wisdom in soil,
The power of a quiet day.

We don't need their products,
Their empty promises,
Their plastic lives.
We need the earth,
We need our people,
We need the roots we've forgotten.

Stop buying,
Stop scrolling,
Stop consuming,
Stop conforming.

Reclaim your time,
Reclaim your health,
Reclaim your power.
Grow something—
Not just food,
But self-respect,
Community,
Purpose.

The change begins when you say enough.
It begins when we turn off the noise,
And start listening to the real world.

SILENT REVOLT

The Truth They Fear

We are many.
We outnumber them.
The ones who pull the strings,
Who hide in the shadows,
Behind walls of glass and steel.

They count on us staying small,
Divided, distracted.
So long as we fear each other,
So long as we fear the unknown,
They keep their hold.

But if we look,
If we see the threads,
The puppet master's hands shaking
Behind their silken curtain,
If we speak out,
One voice at first,
Then two,
Then a thousand,
A million.

They are afraid of us.
Not because of the power they wield,
But because they know
When we realize we are many,
When we stand together,
Their game is over.

They use fear to keep us quiet,
To make us small,

SILENT REVOLT

To make us believe we are powerless.
But fear is their tool,
Not our truth.

We can see through it.
We can hear the lies they tell,
The ones who wear smiles,
But whose hands are stained with control.

It starts with one,
And then another,
And before they know it,
The walls crumble,
The strings snap,
The puppet falls.

And in that moment,
We remember—
We are many.
We always were.

SILENT REVOLT

The Myth of Progress

They tell us progress means change,
But change to what?
The destruction of our neighborhoods?
The hollowing of our communities?
The killing of small businesses?
The flood of people who do not care,
Who take without giving?

Progress is a lie when it leaves behind
Broken lives,
And families lost.

What's "progress" if it's built on blood?
What's change when it erases who we were?

Stop following.
Start doing.
Start protecting what's yours.
Your family, your culture, your values.
The work you do with your hands—
That's where the future lies.

SILENT REVOLT

Rising from the Silence

Truth is buried beneath layers of lies,
Shaped to fit a narrative that doesn't serve us.
We are told what to think, what to say,
What to buy, what to eat.

But they cannot control our thoughts forever.
They cannot hold us in the cage of consumerism.

The world is loud,
But the truth is quiet.
It's in the garden,
In the workshop,
In the books we read,
In the hands that build,
In the people who wake up and say enough.

It begins small,
With one choice—
One refusal—
One voice.

Stand tall.
Choose wisely.
Refuse to comply.
And when we all stand together,
The truth will break free.

SILENT REVOLT

The Smart Phone Blues

Oh, the joy of a smartphone,
A tiny screen that whispers,
"Stare at me, I'm smarter than you!"
And yet, somehow,
I've never felt more alone.

Instagram tells me how great everyone's life is,
While TikTok reminds me I'll never dance
Like a teenager on caffeine and confidence.
But instead of joy,
It leaves me with a sense of loss—
Like I'm watching a parade
But forgot to bring snacks.

So I made a choice—
A bold, rebellious one.
I'll only follow things that make me feel good,
Like motivational quotes and pictures of puppies,
The occasional plant in a sunbeam.
If it's not feeding my soul,
It's getting blocked—
Goodbye, negativity,
I'll never miss you.

But wait—what if I told you,
I'm planning to go even further?
No more mindless scrolling,
No more endless notifications.
I'm getting rid of the smart phone
For a dumb phone—
The kind that just calls, texts, and plays music,

SILENT REVOLT

Like a rebellious flip phone from 2004.

Yes, flip phones are making a comeback!
And no, they're not smart,
But they know their place.
They don't tell you how to live your life—
They just ring, and you pick up!
No apps, no distractions, no filters.
Just good ol' fashioned texting,
Where you press buttons and wonder
Why you ever used emojis.

The irony is that the smart phone,
That "life-enhancer" we all swore by,
Has turned us all into zombies,
Eyes glued to screens,
Minds numb from endless data.
So here's my rebellion:
I'm going back to dumb.

Let's bring back appliances that do exactly what they're meant to—
Washing machines that wash,
Toasters that toast,
And phones that—wait for it—make calls.
It's a revolution, folks.
I'm not lonely;
I'm just selectively social,
And I'm done letting technology run the show.

SILENT REVOLT

The Carbon Conspiracy

Oh, the carbon lies,
Slick as oil on water,
"Cut back, save the Earth!" they say,
But only if you pay the price.
They tell you, "Recycle, save the world!"
While packaging your dreams in plastic shrink-wrap,
Eco-fees tacked on every product,
Because apparently you're the problem here.

But let's talk about the real pollution,
Not the plastic bottle in your kitchen sink,
But the billionaire in his shiny yacht,
Sailing past the melting ice—
He's exempt from the rules, you see,
Because profits don't recycle.
It's all about the bottom line,
While they strip the Earth of its resources,
And send poor souls into deadly mines,
To dig for riches they'll never see.
Their labor and lands—
Exploited for their gain.

Carbon emissions? Oh, they're real,
But not for the CEOs,
No, they're too busy flying jets,
And building empires on the backs of others,
While telling you to reduce your footprint,
By buying the latest "eco-friendly" gadget—
Made in sweatshops, naturally.
The irony is delicious, isn't it?
Buy more to save less.

SILENT REVOLT

The plastic mountains pile higher,
With every product that's wrapped like a gift,
Except it's not for you,
It's for them—the kings of trash,
Who burn the waste when they claim they recycle,
Turning your conscientious effort into smoke.
Oh, it's all a ruse,
A shiny new tax on your poor,
While they profit from the very pollution
They say they're fighting against.

So, yes, go ahead—
Recycling bins stacked to the sky,
Reduce, reuse, recycle,
But if there's no profit in it,
They'll just burn it all—
And charge you for the privilege.
Because in the end,
It's not about saving the Earth,
It's about saving their wallets
While you carry the burden of their lies.

And when the truth breaks through,
And the tides shift,
They'll still sell you beachfront villas,
Made from "sustainable" palm trees—
But don't worry, it's only plastic.

SILENT REVOLT

The Health Revolution

Oh, the world of plastic—
That clingy, toxic, sneaky little villain!
Where phthalates hide in every crevice,
Leaching into your food like uninvited guests.
But fear not, my friends,
There's a simple way out—
Just leave that plastic nonsense,
And embrace the future of…
Glass, steel, and wood, for your health's sake!

Say goodbye to air fresheners,
Those artificial puffs of "clean air"—
Who needs "lavender breeze"
When you could just open a window,
Or maybe enjoy the real smell of your house?
Throw away the chemicals,
You'll breathe deeper, feel better,
And if the environment benefits—well, that's just a bonus.

Now, when you heat your food—
Do not microwave it in that plastic trap!
Use glass, please, or paper towels—
No phthalates, no BPA, just safety.
Cook your meals with care,
Stainless steel, cast iron, copper—
Real materials,
Not that sad, peeling Teflon nonsense.

Throw out those plastic measuring spoons,
You deserve better, like metal,
Not something that warps with time

SILENT REVOLT

And adds "flavors" you didn't sign up for.
Get yourself a solid, reliable set of real tools,
For cooking that actually nourishes you.

Wax paper's your friend,
Plastic is the enemy—
If it doesn't come from nature,
It's not invited.
That plastic-wrapped styrofoam meat packet?
Leave it behind, use some butcher paper,
It's healthier for you—and the bonus?
It's a little kinder to the world.

And water—don't even get me started,
You deserve clean water,
Not plastic-laced toxins.
Filter it with carbon,
For your body's sake.
It's like a little detox with every sip,
And if the planet smiles back,
Well, that's just a happy side effect.

So here's the deal:
Toss out the fake stuff,
The toxic, the flimsy, the harmful—
Choose what's real,
What's solid,
What will nourish you from the inside out.
Your health deserves the best—
And if the environment gets a lift,
That's just a sweet bonus.
You're investing in you,
And the planet might just thank you later.

SILENT REVOLT

The Choice is Ours

The world tells us what to buy,
What to wear, what to eat,
But the truth is, we can decide,
To break free from this deceit.

Stop scrolling for approval,
Stop buying what you don't need,
Start living by your own truth,
Not by the greed they breed.

SILENT REVOLT

Wake Up to Your Power

Stop listening to the noise,
The influencers who sell you lies.
Your voice is louder than their choice,
Wake up to what you can realize.

Knowledge is a key,
In every book, in every mind,
Take time to learn, to set yourself free,
And leave the chaos behind.

SILENT REVOLT

The Power of Less

We've been taught to consume,
To buy, to want, to take,
But true wealth is in what you don't need—
The choices you forsake.

Less stuff, less clutter,
More time, more peace,
More moments spent in living,
Less chasing, more release.

SILENT REVOLT

Rebuild from the Roots

To heal, we must go back,
To simpler, truer days,
Where hands shaped their own world,
And time moved at its own pace.

Grow your food, make your clothes,
Fix what's broken with your hands,
Be the change you've waited for,
In your own home, on your own land.

SILENT REVOLT

The Path Forward

It's not in grand gestures,
or waiting for a savior.
It's in the quiet moments
when we stop playing their game—
unlearning the rules they taught,
and taking back what was always ours:
the right to decide.

We can grow our food,
make our own tools,
and learn to live in harmony,
not against the earth.
We reclaim our health,
choose what we put inside our bodies,
and what fills our minds.

Change comes
when enough of us
create from within,
build community instead of systems,
nourish each other
rather than consume.

No need to shout
or march through the streets.
The loudest change happens
in the small, quiet choices
we make every day,
when we turn off the noise
and listen to our own hearts.

SILENT REVOLT

We can choose to stop
chasing things that don't matter,
to reject endless consumption,
and stop letting our worth
be measured by what we own.

It begins with a question:
What do I truly need?
The answer won't be found
in ads or social feeds,
but in the stillness,
where we can hear
the wisdom of our own hands.

ABOUT THE AUTHOR

Drew Mackby Sand is a Canadian artist and writer whose literary journey began with his first publication while still in his teens. This early success ignited a lifelong passion for exploration in both his artistic and academic pursuits. Equipped with several art degrees and a diverse career across various creative fields, Drew has remained dedicated to his artistic passions. His writing and poetry, chosen as his primary means of deep self-expression, reflect his unique perspective as a self-described black sheep. Through his evocative and heartfelt poetry, Drew connects profoundly with readers, capturing the essence of his experiences and reflections. With a genuine and imaginative spirit, he invites readers to embark on a journey through the rich landscapes of his creative work.

www.ingramcontent.com/pod-product-compliance
Lightning Source LLC
Chambersburg PA
CBHW070429010526
44118CB00014B/1963